MAN AT THE ICE HOUSE

Alison Mace has written poetry all her life, more extensively since abandoning full-time teaching. She has three adult daughters. She lives in the Forest of Dean, but spent the whole of her working life in Yorkshire, whose speech rhythms echo in her work.

MAN AT THE ICE HOUSE

ALISON MACE

The High Window

First published in the UK in 2019 by The High Window Press
3 Grovely Close
Peatmoor
Swindon
SN5 5SN
Email: abbeygatebooks@yahoo.co.uk

The right of Alison Mace to be identified as the author of this work has been asserted by her in accordance with Copyright, Designs and Patent Act, 1988.
© Alison Mace 2019
ISBN: 978-1-913201-13-5

All rights reserved. No part of this book may be reproduced or transmitted in any form or by any means, electronic or mechanical, including photocopying, recording, or by any information storage and retrieval system, without permission in writing from the copyright owner. This book may not be lent, hired out, resold or otherwise disposed of by way of trade in any form of binding or cover other than that in which it is published, without prior consent of the publishers.

Designed and typeset in Palatino Linotype
by The High Window Press.
Cover art © Linda Schwab 2019
Photograph of Alison Mace on back cover © Michael Edwards 2019
Printed and bound by Lulu.com.

In memory of Anne Cluysenaar

CONTENTS

THE UNWRITTEN POEM

The Unwritten Poem   11
The Beautiful Young   12
Bird-boned   13
A Glimpse of Eve   14
Violin Mondays   15
One-night Stand   16
The Sea Kitchen   17
No Hero   18
Perfected   20
'How the sick leaves reel down in throngs!'   22
Water   23
Released   24
At the Airport   25
Tarn Lane   26
Cusp   28

HILDA'S NEW ENGLAND

The Twenty-nine-hour Day   33
June 1904   35
Setting at Odds her Style   36
Twin Sons in Age (i, ii)   38
Man at the Ice House   40
Maine Coast Widow   44
Scattering Will   46
Acres of Diamonds   49

MOTHER, DAUGHTER, FATHER

Months to be Born   53
Washing   54
The Ten Days Stay   55
Birthday Present   56
Sonnets for my Mother (i, ii)   57
Meeting the Child   58
Sorry   59
We Didn't Say   60
Patient to Therapist   61
Nothing to Say   62
Salvatore Culora   64
Butfor   65

AFTER SUMMER

School-teaching (i-vi)   69
Made up   75
My House   76
This Moment   77
Loiterpin, Blakeney Hill   78
At Agios Neofitos   79
Idol   80
On This Day   81
Skunk, Fox   82
Here's Love   84
After Summer   86

THE UNWRITTEN POEM

The Unwritten Poem

I've been writing this poem the whole of my life – or have meant to:
in spring, when it's dandelion week, new green lights hedges,
and yellow fields in their brightness spring up round all horizons,
when clocks have skipped an hour, and I feel like skipping too,
and the sun's been three months climbing and now gives out real heat –
trees gather their shadows to them and cast their portraits down
life-size on pavement, roadway, grass and the Forest paths.

Their limbs and their fingers wreathe and twist – whole, lovely trees,
their noble height and their strength and their delicate tracery, spread
at my feet, a marvel – no more must I squint up into the sun
at them, bleak against dazzling sky; they're gentle, meandering, soft,
and I am invited to walk in their branches, among them and through.
Entranced, I wander across each image, unique in its beauty;
see, as they slip behind, more riches lying ahead.

Yes, every miraculous April I live for short-shadowed trees,
knowing that here is a poem, demanding to be written.
But poems require a dimension this lacks – beyond description,
beyond any simple recording of beauty laid out before me,
or straining attempt to set down the feelings it rouses me to –
something to nail the experience down, a link – some seed
to plant in minds, hoping that it may thrive there and bloom.

So nothing is done, and spring after spring the leaf-buds, flower-buds
swell in the sun, break out. Tree-shadows plump up, hung
with balls, like baubles at Christmas; petals drift down, then seeds
fly on the wind, and a trillion leaves are steadily thickening.
Fresh pale green in May, now they grow dark, opaque.
Shadows crowd closer to trunks. This joined-up solid shade
is welcome when sun beats hot. But my poem stays unwritten.

The Beautiful Young

So beautiful, the young:
a gift I guess we all had,
too driven, rushed, to realise
it wasn't permanent.
Your oyster all before you
you took your pearly skin,
your shining hair, for granted.
Oyster-shell changed for tortoise,
your neck betrays the truth.
Should you retract, and hide it?
Never! This dented armour's
a proof of battles won,
your loosening skin a garment
that suits you more securely
than when it fitted close;
and eyes defy their wrinkles
to flash with love or fire
brilliant now as ever.
And what is past of action
you gain as memory.

So am I now persuaded?
What would I give for magic
to take me back to twenty?
– question without an answer.

Bird-boned

The old woman I caught by her shoulders
lightly skittering sideways
among the wind-bent crowd
just off the bus by the theatre
was only bird-bones in skin
and a frail scared smile.

My daughter told me, she whistled,
gathering coat-wings round her,
it wasn't fit – I shouldn't leave the house –
but I'd my shopping to do . . .

Gently I stood her upright. Released,
Thanks, love, she warbled thinly
and blew away into the precinct
five inches above the ground.

A Glimpse of Eve

Three weeks breathing now, Eve,
twenty-one days in a box
under a measured glow.
Thirty-six weeks today,
that's what the nurses say,
so another four to go
before you can start to live:
shouldn't have smelt the air
till a day beyond New Year.

Your tiny pulsing weight
I lift, invited, and lay
you down, unwrapped, on the bed:
hot red torso, distended,
limbs like fingers and thumbs.
Your legs spring into the cross
of the foetal diagram
'Your Baby at 36 Weeks' –
I glimpse the child unborn.

You seek about, the mouth
wide in your turning head.
Last week you learnt to suck;
now I've given you back
you feed with an earnestness
that shows you mean to grow.
Eve, claiming your future:
whole woman in waiting,
exquisite miniature.

Violin Mondays

Mondays she's here, tiptoe to reach the bell,
inside, removing her shoes as she does at home.
But after we've played we'll be in another room,
the barn. 'Keep 'em on,' I say, 'you might as well.'
She's musical, this child, but she doesn't practise.
Her mum cajoles – begs – bribes – but it's never done.
I don't mind: what she needs is to have some fun
– a game, a laugh, no pressure – to hell with progress.
It's rarely an eight-year-old has known, thank God,
her best friend killed, and her adults, all in shock,
silent and stalled. On Mondays, sometimes, she'll talk
of Charlie – how she thinks about her in bed.
I'm honoured. Me, I had no one, anywhere,
who'd give. So Mondays are good, for me and her.

One-night Stand

  i Sharing the lychee

His sharp knife grates
across the knobbled rind:
pierced, sliced to the stone.
Wet translucent flesh
shows white – fragrant, cool –
slides on their twinned tongues.

  ii Aubade

Stale breath of the bistro
seeps out as she passes:
garlic, tomato, crust.

The whole baking
shifts in the slack gut
of last night's lover sleeping,

its risen dough,
sharp herbal tang,
zest, style, steam

all settled to sludge
shunting on downward,
effluent brewing.

The bistro breathes.
She won't pause long;
just keeps on going.

The Sea Kitchen

To eat or to be eaten
at the sea kitchen's deep stone tables where
cool flow lays straight the drifting, living legumes
among bright fruits, rejoicing jellies –
eat, or be eaten, is the same:
it is the sea kitchen's way.
There is no waste here, and no death.

No Hero

Did you hear of the man who gave
his right arm for his kids? I'll tell you.
He sailed, one night too rough
for the job (but you have to eat)
out through the coastal swell
to the rolling lobster-buoys.

In a buffeting offshore wind
he grapples the line, engages
the powerful winch, switches on –
when – darn! – a gust takes the cuff
of his oilskin, flaps it free
right into the jaw of the winch –
the winch, the winch! It gobbles
his fingers, his palm, his wrist . . .
and the sea and the whistling gale
tumble him overboard. Then,
sprawled in the slapping surf,
alive to the nearness of death,
he sees – though he can't say how –
his children, his girls, in the spray,
clambering on to his boat
to be near him, all three. And now
he knows what to do. With a heave
of impossible strength, his weight
is somehow back on the deck,
his sharpest knife in his hand,
the one that slices rope
clean through . . . and it's done, and he steers
pumping blood, for the shore. Please God,
he prays, don't drown me now.

Back on the beach, this June,
skimming stones for the girls left-handed,
he tells the camera, mildly,
'I guess that's a sensible price
to pay, to be there for your kids –
wouldn't any parent agree?'
His glasses flash, as he leans
to his youngest. Into the lens
he grins, and she drags him to play.

Perfected
*remembering Lesley,
whom spring overwhelmed*

Effaced by winter, they're
ignorable, like her; latent,
brewing a sharp sap.

Ride past them: nothing-trees,
no-counts, inert. But wait.
In cold March pain starts rising

when daffodils' cool trumpets
blare, then go chewed-orange;
excitable tulips fall.

Sticks flash alive – forsythia,
crude acrylic splashes
blinding-April-bright.

Then May, magic with danger:
treacherous hawthorn, blackthorn –
bitter sloes in waiting.

Now horse-chestnut flares,
wastes, gives place to prickles.
Lilac blooms, browns.

Ride by again. Wherever
you go now, look, laburnum
leaps into focus – there

leans over walls to claim
Heptonstall hill; is also
here, in the stonebound park.

Laburnum, its fires, its weeping
inverted candles, hung
from scabbards innocent-green,

lovely, ingenuous,
setting a scene for action,
beauty with menaces.

And she, dumb winter done,
eloquent finally
effects a consummation

terrible as its gold,
laburnum-blatant
with a legacy of poison.

'How the sick leaves reel down in throngs!'
Thomas Hardy, 'During Wind and Rain'

They were fading, failing, once the year turned, and now it is time,
every day shorter, darknesses cooling: time to let go.
Glory of flowering gone, then fruiting, seeding, and even
their reign of gold is waning. They wither and thin, stems shrinking
around their fuses, the tongue-points, and now, with a light wind rising,
the first of them start to come spiralling down, today by tens,
with a breath of frost by thousands, down to the earth they shaded.

From the beginning, when rising spring warmed trunk, warmed twig
and the tree put out its first pale hands to spread to the sun
they were aging, spending themselves to repay the life they sipped,
toughening, pouring back strength down the clean core to the root.
The job's done. Now they will rustle, then rot and settle, drawn back,
mysterious alchemy, to the dark, to be earth again,
their memorial gift a bright new ring at the tree's girth.

Water

trickles among rocks,
deepens, becoming lively,
and gathering strength, divides the land;

sets millwheels turning,
wool spinning, weaving,
Cragside's miraculous lights shining;

can sweep away bridges,
pluck you from a promenade,
beach unwary fish with a mischievous wave,

and can mount past
a swamped car's window
so that there's no more opening doors;

yet, sometimes tranquil, show
your ghost self in a still pool:
smile, Narcissus! – but know
one drop can shatter you.

Released

Wherever it is she's gone,
wherever the spark of her fled
after it struggled free
of tortured, poisoned flesh
and the contrary compulsion
to keep on taking breath,
we have this to be thankful for:

no more loving her through
that cough, the effort to sleep,
later, to stay awake;
and awake, the need to smile.
The gasping catch in her voice,
the treacherous morphine pump –
banish them, thrust aside
all memory of her pain,
pain of a magnitude
we cannot comprehend,
we who are whole, or nearly,
and drawing breath at will.
That nagging minor ache
as we bent to hear her whisper
does not appear at all
on the scale of her long enduring.

And so at last we are glad,
we find ourselves rejoicing
at her release. All over.
The time is not quite yet
when a version of our friend
in her busy, vivid youth
will flash in our brains and show
what she, and we, have lost.

At the Airport

Will the end be like this? – stepping
quite confident from outside air
to queue for treatment? – queuing, then reaching
the expert who'll assess your case and bear
your burdens away, you may not notice
that you've surrendered – dazed by the lights, the noise,
the importance; scanned, you're left to lounge in what is,
really, the halfway house to a loss of choice.
So you're waiting, trapped, never knowing how long
till your personal flight is called, even now –
rigidly calm above the panic rising,
able to think of nothing but when, and how
your call to the tunnel will come, or where
you'll go, catapulted upward through cloud into thin air.

Tarn Lane

Well, riding the bumps
from Keighley Tarn to the end
where the road swings down to Goose Eye
or right-then-left on the Pole Road
to Cowling Pinnacles –
riding the bumps – remember? –
is only what we all did
sometimes, when we were young
and didn't have to be sensible
all of the time.

And these were young,
the six boys who did it
a June evening lately –
only schoolkids still,
the four crammed in the back –
the young man driving older,
twenties, married, a father,
but lad enough to be happy
to show off, give them a thrill,
take the old Astra swooping
up each tarmac crest,
taking off ('We're flying!')
then graunching back to earth,
scoring a new scar
on the long-suffering road.

This morning, alongside
the deepest dip, it seems
some lout's been dumping here –
paper and stuff on the verge –
till we look closer, see
that what we're gently passing,
mounting the rise with caution,

are flowers, laid for the boys
who rode the Keighley bumps
recklessly one still evening;
sun burying itself in the fields,
stars lying in wait for them,
the car flung over and over.

Cusp
a poem for the spring equinox

The old year dead, we shiver,
pull curtains close, shut out
the slowly lengthening dusks,
the fine dry twigs for kindling
that fall in gales, and clear
the trees for new plump buds.
Hiding indoors we miss
snowdrops that brave the frost
and tight short catkins, waiting.

Winter is long. We strain,
longing for early light,
willing the sun to rise
the daily fraction sooner,
left, towards due east.
The short month's wished away
in dreams of summer skies.
Catkins are quietly stretching,
daffodils peer unnoticed.

March, and the days grow fast:
we speed with the sun through Pisces,
never taking thought
that once Fish turns to Ram
we'll cruise towards the solstice
and on through fading August;
then to the fall of the leaves,
shuddering dank November
and down again to dark.

So rise in a chill dawn:
meet the brisk March breeze,
stride over fields of plough
as darkness warms to pearl,
as sun tints earth with rose,
to see the brown hares run.
Stand on the point of balance,
winter to spring, and know
its live pulse as it passes.

HILDA'S NEW ENGLAND

The Twenty-nine-hour Day

In mid-Atlantic trance
child who used to be me
stood up and pointed back
at visiting Aunt Hilda,
eldest of eight, who'd crossed
the sea we're crossing now
when she was still a girl,
even before my father
and two more brothers were born.
I knew her history,
I dreamt of her three sons,
my cousins, never seen,
heard of their marriages,
their children's births, their homes.
It was my high romance;
I longed for Christmas Cove,
their summer home in Maine,
but never thought to go there.
The years have passed, these boys
are in their seventies
now that we're in the sky,
flying above the ocean,
closer every hour.

And now we stir and wake –
  half –wake . . . and land, and stumble
    into a lighted place.
      Glass eye on a stalk
        scanning ours in turn
         suspects of the Union
           then Alamo's tough dame:
             'If *she*'s gonna drive
               it's eight a day extra'. . .

Signs few and sudden
  road at last found
    1A North of Boston
      out to Geoffrey's Neck
        white house by the marsh
        welcomed in by strangers

The twenty-nine-hour day
  eddies round a basin
    round, down, away

Deep pillow at Tab's
  new house at the shore
    counting love in clouds
      piling round the bed
        cheek to pulsing neck
          runnels through the marsh
          salt pools rise and fall

June 1904

Hilda, not yet sixteen – does her bold heart quake? –
is steaming towards her new world, and her old
bachelor uncle, who's undertaken to make

a lady of her. Oh, he has been told,
in letters from Bristol, England, about this head-
strong niece: loud, selfish – shaming! – cannot be held,

sets her sister and three young brothers at odds:
defies her father, Walter; scorns the irate
pleas of poor Anna, her mother – whose tentative words

to stern, important Harry indicate
her own condition: another child expected –
and that being so, much better not to wait

but send Hilda soon and let her be instructed,
pray God the school of Harry's choice can save
the girl from the ruin the Bristol one's predicted.

He waits on the dock to receive her: bearded, grave.

Setting at Odds her Style

Setting at odds: her style, her destiny.

Shortish and plump, white hair swept up, a mouth
complacent and pugnacious both at once –
I see Aunt Hilda, in my teenage years,
setting at odds her family 'back home'.
She always stayed with us. My grandmother
expected it – though it's a close-run thing
which of them loathed these charged encounters more.
One visitation was the only time
I heard my father shout: I asked him something –
nothing important – as he stepped indoors.
'Give me a chance!' he thundered, then slammed down
a basketful of Brussels sprouts he'd picked,
escaping down the garden to avoid
his womenfolk – Grandma in angry tears,
his sister Edith in her room, offended,
me, roasting chicken for a gruesome feast
and Hilda, coolly dashing off a score
or so of letters to her 'dearest friends'
back in Northampton, Mass.

Here, at the Maine coast cottage Harry built
the year she came, and left her when he died –
knocked from a kerb one foggy night – his haven,
where every summer she'd kept house for him
and met her husband on his stony beach –
here on their bluff, I mention casually
to neighbours calling by, that I can sense
her presence in the house. And they recoil! –
recover – make a joke of it – pass on.

Setting at odds her twins, Wilfrid and Talbot,
named for a Bristol brother and her husband,
'Tab is a *maker*,' she'd declare, 'and Will,
alas, a *breaker*.' So she set their sails,
and winds have brought them where they are today:
Tab's mouth is cradled now in smiling-lines;
querulous Will's – his double – sadly droops.

At odds with Talbot senior, she took
the twins, and little Norman, her delight,
to Paris for divorce, some time between
the Great War and the next. Then, on a trip
back to New York, weary of twins, she left
them there with her successor, steaming back
to France with Norman only.

                          He repaid
her favours: he and Barbara took her on,
cared for her all the decades of her age
in their own home, and amicably fielded
her idiosyncratic brand of wit:
'Hilda, I'd rather not be called a bitch.'
'Oh, sorry, dear; I *will* try to remember . . .'
But long before she made her century
she'd 'sold' her precious cottage to them both
for 'love, affection and one dollar'. So
it is that they're our hosts this August week.

But Will does not forgive her.

Twin Sons in Age

i Massachusetts: Tab

Tab makes slow coffee, hazy
who's had some, hasn't, or
quite who these house-guests are,
which of us is his kin.
Not sure either if this,
his house in Ipswich, Mass.,
close by the marsh, across
the way from his nephew Sam's
is where he'll be this winter,
or whether the one in Wellesley
he loved for fifty years
is sold or not, or what
to give the guests for breakfast.

ii Vermont: Will

What is the plan this evening?
 - thin query on the line.
And why am I excluded?
  Surely we made it clear?
Alice, are you coming?
  Not till the morning now.
Nobody fixed me dinner.
  Jody was just arriving,
  wasn't she? – as we left.
We're going out for dinner?
  Tomorrow. Somewhere special,
  if he can manage stairs.
Waiter, this steak's like leather.
  We'd better take him home . . .
where, reaching down a volume
of Robert Frost, he reads
aloud to us for hours,
fluent, relaxing, smiling,
right till we have to go
– and possibly continues
until the bedtime carer
comes softly in at ten.

Man at the Ice House
for Norman, with a bow to Frost

'Nathan! Who is that man – you know the one,
we've passed him often, and we did today
driving from Damariscotta to your mother's?
He stands beside that barn, a mile or two
from – where? South Bristol, that's the place.'

                                              'Ah, yes,
I know the man you mean. His name is Hamlin –
lives at that cottage right above the beach,
Juniper Knoll – the house among the trees,
that looks straight out across the Thread of Life.
Why do you want to know so much about him?'

'He looked – I can't explain – he looked as if
he had a purpose, more than just the run
of summer people do, vacationers –
is that the word? He looked committed, somehow.
But anyway, he's old – he'll be retired?'

'Old? Well, I guess. Not young, at any rate.
His mother, *she* was old. I can remember
old Hilda Hamlin, quite a character.
She sowed those lupines all around the headland,
or so the story goes, and I believe it.
She owned that place, her uncle had it built –
an English guy, your countryman in fact –
philosophy his subject, I believe,
anyway a professor, Mom would tell me,
highly respected at his college, too.
But even Mom's too young to know all this
herself: I guess she heard it as a kid.
Hilda had made a hundred when she died,
more, even; I forget; she wasn't here

her last few summers. Well, she lived with him -
Norman, his name is – and his wife – Barbara,
that's right. They cared for Hilda till she died,
at home, their home, down-Maine, Brunswick, I think,
and now they have the summer place themselves.
Their kids come too, and *theirs* – they're mostly grown.
So yes – he must be quite an age by now,
your Norman that you noticed. What's the thing
that struck you so about him?'

                        'Well, you know,
that look of purpose, as I said. What *is*
that place, the barn-like building where we see him,
a barn with steep-pitched roofs that almost meet
the ground on either side? – a pond behind,
I think – I glimpsed some water.'

                        'Yes, you're right,
it's coming back to me. A pond is right.
The barn's an ice house (something you won't know,
coming from England?) – always was, years back.
Now Norman Hamlin and his pals have put it
back to the way it was. It's running now . . .
Lizzie, I guess we'll get the car and go there,
it's worth a visit.'

                   'Ice? You mean, like, cold?
In August? Don't you mean in spring, before
the sun gets hot and melts it? Not by now!'

'Didn't you see that box out front? They sell
their ice from June to when the summer folk
are driven home by cold and dark October.
I guess there's some left over even then –
there's surely ice there now. They insulate
the walls – you know? They're packed with - is it sawdust?

Then, on the ice, they spread this saltmarsh hay –
has to be saltmarsh hay, it has no seeds –
to keep it cold inside.'

                    'The walls? There's barely
a yard or so of wall below that roof –'

'Not those walls, no. The ice is in a block,
like a huge cube, between the inner walls,
a cube made up of smaller cubes packed close.
The side-rooms help. They've made those a museum
for ice-picks, rakes and such, the apparatus
(it's savage-looking stuff, all spikes and hooks)
they use for harvesting the chunks of ice
they cut out of the pond.'

                    'That pond I saw?
They *harvest*? When? In winter-time?'

                            'That's right.
They come in February, so I'm told,
using a plow to get here through the snow,
and carve it out in blocks. You'll see – they have
the pulley system still, the same they used
in the old days, before refrigeration.'

'Pond-water! – and they sell ice from this box
in front? That's wonderful! Let's buy some, Nate.
We've got that old machine your granny left,
the one you said made ice-cream. Turn the handle –
isn't this right? – and churn the mixture round
until it hardens up? It wouldn't matter
what kind of ice was packed in round the edges.'

'It doesn't anyway, that pond's so pure.
It's tested every year, it's always sweet –

it's fed by springs. The more they take away
each winter for the ice house, why, the more
there is next year. The springs keep filling it.'

'I like that thought. I want to see it all.
And aren't we nearly there? Why do you think
this Norman Hamlin does it still? That journey
must be a brute in winter. And it takes –
surely it takes some strength to do that work,
heaving the blocks up? How, when the layers are in
two-thirds, or more, of the distance to the roof –?'

'The pulleys see to that. But yes, you're right,
Lizzie, it's work for young, strong men. I guess
he likes to know it went on all those years
his mom, and uncle – great-uncle, I mean –
were living at the cove? Keeps him young, maybe,
being involved in keeping all that going.'

'Perhaps. Yes, that's the way of it. And look,
he's here still – busy knocking in a post.
What does the notice say?'

      '*An Ice-Cream Social*,
that's what it says. This Thursday. Shall we go?
They hold one every summer, like the folk
way back, who used to sell his mother ice.
We'll go, and meet our neighbors. And who knows,
with luck we'll see the ghost of Hilda Hamlin.
For now I'll introduce you to her son.'

Note: Pictures of activities at the Thompson Ice House, South Bristol, Maine, can be found online via Google.

Maine Coast Widow
for Barbara Hamlin

My feet know every root and rocky turn
from here to our quiet road – Route 129
you followed till it ended, as roads must
that thread our bony-finger headlands. So
you're here! I'm here! and welcome!

       This is my first
summer alone here. I had never thought
how much he shared with me – the work, I mean;
I knew we shared our lives. Sixty-one years
I was his wife, starting at still-nineteen.
And this has been the worst year of my life.
And yet – it's odd – I've kind of come of age,
somehow, since Norman died. I know my mind
more surely now. I know I'd never choose
to leave our house in Brunswick – know I must,
sometime, and this one too: a summer guest,
that's all I'll be, assisted up that path
my soles know every slant of. But that's good:
I'll get to gaze out on the Thread of Life,
Monhegan Island in its haze of mist,
his mother's 'diamonds' twinkling from the water,
the lobster-fishers . . . and I'll think about
the day we scattered Norman's ashes there,
from boats, as he decreed.

       I'll sell the house
in Brunswick. Oh, I like it very much,
my house, but I can live without it well
so long as I can stay around my town,
go to my book-club, church, enjoy my friends,
get out to parties sometimes; read, and cook –
but only when I want to. I shall join

that sensible community The Oaks,
right in the town there, where I'll get some care
when the time comes for it – but that's not yet –
and never lose my freedom. Not for me
a house across the way from family –
a cage roped off from all I know, my life
sinking behind, only my kids for friends;
and too much energy spent trying hard
to get it right with them: not ask too much,
not thank too little, or be there too much . . .
and watch, so helpless, as all that gets worse
and I can see the strain across their faces
until I won't see even that. And then
their guilt at sending me away to where
I know no face at all, and can't retain
a new one for a minute.

                     No. I know
where I am bound – not to where 129
gives way to dirt, then rocks, and after those
the ocean, reaching out to meet the sky.
I could be traveling backward, but I'll take
this same road to a life I'll call a new one –
old friends, new friends; responsibilities
shed from me like old skins.

                           I came of age
at eighty, and I'll live my new life through,
a happy childhood time, and I'll stay smiling
all through the years they love me like a baby,
right up until I can't smile any more.

Scattering Will
Maple Hill, Vermont, October 2009

Sunday. We drive to Jody's place. 'My loom . . .
not set up yet, there's stuff with the computer.
My job with Will, that's what has let me buy it.
Wanted to show you that. His cactus also –
see, it's in flower . . .'

                We start across her field:
a Bread & Puppet scarecrow, heaped potatoes,
sun beating fierce and hot; and now we're climbing –
Christopher carrying the heart-shaped box
inside its plastic bag, under his arm –
past apple-trees, through swampy patches, then
under a gate or two, unhitching first
electric fences that will cease to shock,
whether the farmer's switched them off or no,
soon, when the frost-hard ground disables them;
but cows have learned their lesson: they'll stay clear.
A steeper rise – the summit's up ahead –
live tree, bone tree, a low bush and a rock.

Christopher mounts the rock. 'Ash scattered here
when the rain comes to wash it underground
will leach down through the wood, enter the brook'
(ever west-running?) '- pass his house, the town,
go on across the state to Lake Champlain,
then flow out with the river to the ocean.
It's the right place, I think, even if Dad
may never have hiked up here, See, over there'
(sun warming our backs) '- those farthest peaks
may well be Canada. When Will came first
you could see all these mountains from the house.
Then woods rose up around him. But no matter,
he could still see the mountains, all his life.'

'I'm nervous . . . think I know how Jesus felt
before he did the Cross thing.'
                                   'Jody – oh!
– the Cross thing! Well – I guess we all feel that.'

'Take just a little. Where's the wind coming from?
Upwind, and it could blow back in your face.'

'That's Will for you. And – feel – I swear it's warm,
the ash – from climbing up here in the sun?
– or from Chris hugging it? Well. There he goes.'

'I'm going down towards that yellow wood.
A little bit at least of Will should start
its journey in a yellow wood.'
                               But oh,
this process isn't easy. Here's the part,
after all yesterday's acclaims and plaudits –
this pinch of grit between my fingers, loosed
to trickle through dead leaves, with some puffed back,
a film over my sleeve – this is goodbye.

'I'm never going to wash this hand!' Dear Alice,
tomorrow when you have to, it may be
a grain or two of Will can find a home
under your nail for just a little longer.

Shots in the wood; second shots echoing.
 'I'm glad that wasn't happening when we started.'
But now the hunters, though they'll never know it,
are offering Will some last two-gun salutes.
Alice and Jody hug. Chris stands apart.
I sit alone, my back against the rock.

The cold is finding finger-ends and toes:
time to be going down again, now shadows

are stretching out and slanting east. But still
the sun shines bright and friendly. We descend,
back to the day-to-day. Chris picks an apple
to give me, and I bite its ice-white flesh.
Sweet juice starts out. This is Vermont, Will's place,
and here we honour him.
                                 More guns ring round.

Acres of Diamonds
Juniper Knoll, Christmas Cove, Maine

Stand here: it's the only thing my difficult aunt
loved – freely, without the need to scoff
or score - her cove, her cottage. The house stood gaunt

on the headland then, these trees came later. The bluff,
ungrassed, ungardened, dropped to a bouldered shore
and the water, the Thread of Life. Beyond the rough

line of the Ledges, clear days like this, she saw,
as we can now, Monhegan Island afloat
on a pale raft of mist. Those early, raw

years of her exile, she made this garden bright
with lupines, and stripped their pods, and walked the whole
length of the headland, casting seeds about.

Was she making the land hers, feeding her soul
with beauty, to leave the puzzling past behind?
What she waited for, we're told, was this morning fall

of the sun at a certain slant, and a soft wind
coaxing to delicate troughs an azure sea.
Then, she'd laugh with delight at the wealth she owned:

'Acres of diamonds!' Look: her legacy.

MOTHER, DAUGHTER, FATHER

Months to be Born

March: the only one really –
coming to light with the light, the waking year,
Proserpina close by, shaking earth from her hair,
darkness dissolving, the long bright summer to run.

May I can understand:
its dangerous magic, scents
that can send you dizzy, the woods
dappled with heat, beckoning;

October, even: a hunting moon,
first frosts, your footsteps ringing
on the hard planes
of a new early dark.

Those I can respect.
But isn't it universal?
Born in a nest of soused November leaves,
delivered to the dyspeptic fug
of dreg-December – worse, the day itself,
nose put out of joint by baby Jesus –
they still rejoice and bless it?

No, give me Proserpina,
my angular hares boxing
in ploughed fields at dawn,
my delicate, chill cusp.

Washing

Now the thrumming machine has stopped, and I,
tugging it open, scrabble out the clump –
the taut-wound tights strangling a bundled sheet
twisted with shirts and tea-towels – all to hang out.

Out to my garden, the damp load on my hip:
out in another garden, long years gone,
I drubbed my dollies' dresses in soapy water,
My dark-tressed mother standing strong above me,

she stretching up to the line, reaching to peg
her grown-up blouses and cloths and skirts, while I
crouched in the vivid, detailed grass, and squelched
a little world of washing in my bowl.

Rinse it, she said, now rinse it clean – you need
fresh water, love. I got some in my can,
tilted the bowl, saw the rich suds pour out
floating the blades of grass, then slowly sinking.

From can to bowl I splashed a sparkling stream –
but added a bit more soap, just to make sure;
if she saw that, she didn't interfere
and both of us got on with our lovely work.

She does no washing now. My memories
of her stop short, stop dead – too soon, so much
too soon after the washday in the grass.

I've rinsed my grown-up tangle as well as I can.
I'll sort it out and fly it in the sun
in memory of hers.

The Ten Days Stay
The Cock and Rabbit, The Lee, Bucks

Huge wooden Admiral, once a ship's nose,
stares over the green hedge. I am small.
I did not know I was so small, till now.

Two, three, four bells toll from the dark church
the other end of the green. But why
am I awake, awake, as the night goes on?

Doves sound a falling call from the summer trees
behind the pub. I swing. I think. Doves
ought to be nice, but these ones make me sad.

Kind uncle visits me. He looks sad too.
We pull the grasses, strip them, and pull each other's
hair out, laughing. Wonderful relief.

Making meringues. The cook suddenly hugs me.
I'm having a good time. I think I am.
– when did they say my father might be coming?

He came.
        She died, love.
                Oh. So that was it.

Birthday Present

That bottle of ink – black, and its lid
as big as the biscuit on top – plain chocolate,
his favourite, the kid said. We bought them both for her,
the ink and the biscuits – got a smile out of her,
that can't be bad. For his birthday. Her dad.

I can't understand him – hasn't been near her.
It's nearly a fortnight since they had rooms here.
The pair of them left her for us to look after.
Poor kid. Very quiet, these last days. No wonder.

He's come here to tell her. The wife did seem strange.
Well, tense, you know, nervy. But this – well, it's shocking
to think of a mother . . . the child's only eight.

Well he came in the end – yes, he's here, he's outside,
he's packed her off north with his brother, her uncle.
They've just driven off. I'll miss her, I think.

Look, here he comes now, to pick up his presents,
settle his bill. He does look cut up.
Perhaps I won't charge for the bottle of ink.

Sonnets for my mother

i Wartime picnic

The gap in the hedge is thorny, but we're through,
sitting together in long rough grass, a bright
blessing of sunshine everywhere, and you
lying back, laughing, making it all feel right,
forgetting the bombs, your flags across the map,
our house half-full of strangers, and our man
somewhere unknown in Europe. You unwrap
tomatoes, bread – doing the best you can
with home-grown, queued-for, scarce; for me it's bliss
unbounded, the perfect day. Later I see
how brave you were that morning, and why this
is almost my only unstained memory
of you, of us. How soon it came about
that you stopped laughing, and the sun went out.

ii Coming closer

Years later, when my neighbour did it too,
with rope and beam in his case, and his son
came in from school and met him staring – Ben,
his charge, his pride, his pal – I came to know
how all-eclipsing pain can be, and how
this was the way of it for her too, when
she threw her handbag down and faced the train
and leapt out of my world. Learn to allow
such pain more pressing than my need of her.

And now I meet her dreaming. She is young,
smiles gently as I'm trying to explain,
'I'm not a child now – fifty, sixty, more
than you were, mother, ever.' But my song
flows by her, and we shall not meet again.

Meeting the Child

You never know when you may come
face to face with her.
Here she is now, standing in your path,
sturdy, smiling, scuffed leather sandals
and a sundress, yellow blue and white.
How well you remember that –
home-made . . . and if that's what she's wearing
she's not more than seven. So
decide not to speak, not this time –
just smile back and pass on,
don't let her see
your sadness at what will happen, how things
are about to change for her.
Wait for another time
when you find her older, worried,
her shiny hair cut short and badly,
that loving-everyone smile
submerged. This time, let her know
how good she is, how lovely,
and that whatever happens
she will always be lovely inside.
See the smile again. Give her a long hug,
and let her look hard at you, see
that at the far end of her life
smiling will be back, the unique
and flaming essence of her
will have won through, her days
always enriched by friends.
Smile together once more.
Now let her go.
She'll be all right, you know.
Just look at you now.

Sorry

Aunt, I look back at last, and I am sorry,
sorry for how we were, for things we said,
often unkind. We did each other no good.
I grieve now too for your fate: you'd never marry,
your Geoffrey cold under France, your heart a stone
as, smiling, you gave thanks, seeing each young brother
come home unhurt from one war or another.
What longings you must have felt, but could not own.

You took me on, a grieving child, when you
were old and already ill; how hard you tried,
I see now, strove to do right, until you died –
crushed by the weight of all you had to do,
trapped in a mesh of toil, confusion, worry.
I never loved or thanked you. Edith, I'm sorry.

We Didn't Say

I didn't cry. He'd have hated it if I had.
I took control, I was calm, I was sorry for *him*
(but I didn't say) – having to come that day,
his birthday too, to tell me – the thing he said.
But didn't he lie? – 'an accident'? Some bold lad
down Manor Way filled in the gaps for me.

But they stay, the glaring gaps, for me and my dad
to this day: *Road closed. No way.* But I didn't know
he'd actually die, in that silence: we'd speak, one day
of her we both loved? But no. He never did.
And nor did I.

Patient to Therapist

It was a skeleton, and quite a big one.
It flailed its limbs, banged hard against the box,
which trembled. How to contain, not only that
but life, and job, as well? – it was too much.

You drew it out, dismembered, through a slit
only just wide enough; and bone by bone
you laid the terrible corpse out on your bench,
item by item: 'Those were fingers only;
this is a big one, though: here an axe fell –
don't turn your eyes away, it's just one piece,
and fleshless now. Try for the backbone next.
Too big? No matter.'

                So you coaxed them out,
item by item, stubborn bone by bone.
You ranged them neatly. 'There you are,' you said,
'this is the whole collection – there's your bogy!'
That? Was that all? 'That's all it comes to now,
a bundle of sticks, no more; but they're still yours:
remember that, and take them back. You must.
Up with the lid, just stow them in a corner.
They're quiet now, they'll never give much trouble –
just a small extra weight to carry.'
                                  Yes,
a small weight, nothing much. I'll manage. Thank you.

Nothing to Say
with a nod to Sharon Olds

When my father at last came to the Home
because there was nothing more to be done for him,
I came in there unwillingly.
I did not know how I should behave,
I was pleased when the Home's tabby
cat came in too and I
picked up this soft cat and held it above
the high cot sides he was imprisoned in,
and he looked up almost eager,
'Hello, puss,' he said, and I was glad, but he
did not seem to recognise me.
I held his warm feet and knew
they would not be warm for much longer,
and I felt nothing. Not like
that time earlier in the hospital, when
he was better from the urine
infection, but now he had another,
a chest infection, his lungs bubbling,
every breath fighting its way through
a tight pathway of phlegm.
That time he knew me, and he tried to
send his brother his best wishes
in French, as if he knew
communicating now would be tricky, and
thought it might work better if he
dodged the difficult English
language. That time I was suddenly
overwhelmed, filled right up
with certainty that he would die, and
that it might take months,
and that time I cried, and the stern
woman at the nurses' desk
on the way out asked me, 'Why

are you crying, what's the matter?' and there was nothing I could say to her, nothing to say at all.

Salvatore Culora

Loss – how it is sometimes
attended by strange pleasures
woven with regrets:

Sunday, eve of the funeral,
unknown man comes knocking.

'Salvatore Culora –
sorry, I cannot make it
tomorrow – wanted to come –
very good friend to me –
a hospital appointment –
I am so glad to meet you –
he was so proud of you,
told me a lot about you.'

*Salvatore Culora! –
half-obscured by lilies,
ill, with a bandaged face.
Yes! I know of you too –
your unforgettable name
ringing through all my visits
conjures his happy voice.*

I grasp your hand today,
our first and only meeting.

'. . . know he valued your friendship . . .
good luck with your appointment . . .'

Salvatore, greeting.

Butfor

My parents met in their thirties:
she tautly strung, impatient, clever; he
steadier, gentle, lacking in irony.
They did not heed the warning.
But if this had not been,
the mist-filtered sun this morning,
inquisitive cattle breathing
over a wet hedge, the spangled bryony,
those puddles like pearls –
could never have been mine.

AFTER SUMMER

School-teaching
six sonnets for performance

i
A dog, yes, that's what it is, a class new to you –
not dogs, *a dog*, that you're training collectively –
young dog, that would follow instinct and do to you
unthinkable things, if you took it passively
the first time, legs wired to the bell, it rushed
to the door, this puppy, this half-tamed hound – a riot
of bags swung on to backs – chairs, tables pushed-
rocked-kicked to chaos . . . leaving a sudden quiet
resounding with horror. No. If you let that go
you'd be stuck with it for ever. What you do,
if the hound's run loose even once, is haul it home,
oblige it to sit, then calmly let it know
'to heel' is the only way to leave this room.
And the one who gives the go-ahead is you.

ii
You do, just sometimes, begin to wonder why
you stay in thrall to a job like this:
no time for coffee – break duty –
no 'frees' – on cover – so no time for a piss;
not crucial, that, in the light
of meetings at lunchtime, so no chance
anyway for a drink at all, just straight
on through, weaving the weary afternoon dance,
then off again, legging it to some distant hut
for a 'twilight' cramming session before the exams
kick in. Then home – cook a bit, mark a bit – and that,
that breathless hike . . . just about sums
it up. Bedtime. That was your day.
No wonder a third of the teachers stayed away.

iii
Away, some night, on a trip, perhaps to a play –
such a great thing to do, despite the tricky
preamble – money, drop-outs, people away
all morning, all day – but there for the bus if you're lucky –
worth it, to see them have a taste of theatre.
I think of Sofina, lost in Hermione's trial,
turning, huge-eyed: 'How can he *do* this to her?'
Mamillius lost – the girl aghast and pale.
She'll be the one, this time, as we say goodbye
at the dark school gates, to thank us. If no one does,
though, it won't matter. This is me on a high!
It's stuff you don't *have* to do makes teaching buzz.
Home with no marking done and just nine hours
to morning registration. But who cares?

iv
Who *cares*? Well, the Pastoral staff, those specialist folk
who're paid to process angst, and do their best
to soothe it. But kids will go to someone they like,
tell their griefs to a person they know and trust,
and that's their English teacher, often as not,
who's read their poems, who's had a privileged look,
in Drama, at what is eating out a heart –
who understands, from knowing them, how they tick.
And any pretext'll do: 'Miss. I can't
do this York thing. Because he used to take me there,
often. My dad. And it keeps . . . ' He only went
to answer the door. Just slumped across a chair,
dead. Over and over it plays in her brain.
She cries it out. Never talks to me again.

v
Some never speak to me again, ever,
though more of them must know me than I recognise
as we tread our town. The ones who gave most bother,
those are the good 'uns – the ones who told you lies
upon lies, who tied you in knots – they're happy to own
you, later. In Brooks's, looking for fireback clay,
I jump: 'Ey-up, miss, aren't we talkin' then?'
'Marc?' 'Marc Metcalf, aye!' 'And it's Marc with a C,'
I add, and he grins all over. 'Miss – I've got
to apoligise to yer – I know I wa' reight bad
in them days …' No, Marc, no . . . It's really not
for him to say sorry. Because I knew – dear God –
what he had to put up with at home, that lad. And how!
But here he is – through it? – and beaming to see me now.

vi
Now, how many years later? – seventeen
since I fled the full-time slog – do I regret
the treadmill? No. I can't. It's odd, it's germane
to being yourself, or having the kids you've got –
wasn't that a treadmill too? – but one you trod
like breathing, to keep you *you*, to grow, to make
you the person you have to be.
                              But I tell you: God!
I wouldn't do it again, if I could look
forward from when I started. And anyone
who's dear to me, let them keep away from school!
But someone, I guess, has got to drag the young
from child-minded cradle to when they draw the dole?
No. That's brutal. I loved it. But was I free
to live? I was not. That's what I have to say.

Made up

Hope you don't mind me watching from across
the train. Journey-fatigued, I can't stop looking
at all the intricate trouble you've been taking
to make cosmetic adjustments to your face.
You remind me of someone I taught – a tiny lass,
quiet and shy and modest, never seeking
attention – yet something about her raised a sneaking
awareness of lurking wit – so easy to miss.

You, with your flawless matt beige base, the dark
window-frames round your eyes, the soaring lines
of your brows, which give you a look of scared surprise,
and your lips, a brownish red . . . all this just means
you're invented; you've masked the wit, your essential spark.
What will it take to free you from that disguise?

My House
Keighley, Yorkshire, 2006

It likes me, I know, the house,
my Yorkshire house. I've been
the pulse of it, its life through the bright days,
its nightly-ebbing warmth as it drifts with me,
creaking, shifting under its carpet clothes,
relaxing all its joints.
                        It has enjoyed,
surely, my gentle closure of its doors,
neat click, no vulgar bang – sign of respect
between us; and it's preened with pride
in the smart clean coats of paint
I've dressed it in. It has breathed deep
our kitchen – my curries, soups,
my sweet vanilla cake – all wafting
to settle through its fibres.
                        Whose eyes
does it watch through, see the dark line of the moor
meet the changing sky? And whose
are the ears that hear our end-of-summer owls
shriek over its slates, or the Railway Children's
engines whoop from beside the tumbling Worth? –
calls to prayer from the mosque, volleys of fireworks,
crackle of frosty leaves dropping through boughs,
or howl of the winds that fling hard rain in squalls
to course down its rough white face?

Will it be perplexed, my sturdy Yorkshire house,
the day the pack of lifters and looters comes
to gut it, strip it bare and carry out
all it has known me by?
                        Oh, what will it do,
my house, when I prise myself from its embrace
and leave it cold and blind?

This Moment

At this or any moment I tune in –
how many are being born, or uttering
their ultimate rattling breaths, or waiting
in littered doorways, knives at the ready?
Myriad, more than I can contemplate.

Knowledge that's no real knowledge:
the thousands of children a day
dying in rain-starved Africa – that's . . .
how many, at this moment? Too many,
too many by far, for empathy to reach to.

Camping out for the sales, screaming at spouses,
dressing at chill dawn, herding their sheep,
administering the anaesthetic, losing at chess,
knocking on dark doors while the blue light flashes –
all this just splits my brain a million ways.

This moment – now – knows just one focus.
I stare, blank, at the vet's glass baubles
strung along the reception counter.
My cat lies comatose across my lap.
Our turn is next. I am betraying him.

Loiterpin, Blakeney Hill

The sign leans skew-legged on the steep verge:
LOITERPIN – road snaking up round the hill's right shoulder,
fast going back to a track; mud up the middle
grows cushions of grass, soused leaves squelch at the sides.
But Loiterpin fruits, nuts, holly! – always the best
of any about. Picking along the hedge,
caught up by a smiling woman, a wagging dog,
I'm invited: 'Half a mile on, across from our house –
incredible crop this year – those blackberries
just come and come. You're welcome, I can't keep up!'
So I've picked there since, for my jellies, crumbles – till now
I hear she is felled by a stroke – leg, arm, speech, sight . . .
gone into a home, dog and husband left despondent.
Her berries, unpicked, shrunk, petrified, stare across
at a house that today I see is up for sale.
And Loiterpin's nameless, now, the old sign fallen and lost.

At Agios Neofitos

Neofitos, cool in his cell
fourteen feet up rock-face,
too successful,
too much charisma,
hermit with a following,

hollowed the ribbed cliff
much higher up,
safe from his copycats:
the old holes good enough
for their prayers and their paintings.

Today, Neofitos,
gaze down on this booth
where a kind fat Brother,
curled cat on his lap,
takes our eight Euros

for a look at those holes,
their famous Last Suppers
fading on stone,
and tell us whether
you bless or curse us.

Idol

There he'd sit in state, in the big armchair,
children all round him, jostling to have their go,
adoring his wacky tracksuit, his scarecrow hair,
'cos *Jim'll Fix It, for you – and you – and you.*

Nowhere he couldn't enter; always at ease
in celebrity-hospital-porter uniform,
slipping from bed to bed, making their days:
the nation's darling, charity-charmer supreme.

A girl, who'd been fourteen, now fifty and ill,
was interviewed. She told it straight and blunt,
what he made her do as payment for her thrill.
But Auntie wouldn't listen, took no account

of her honesty, her shame, her courage – nor
how he fixed it for ever, for her. *And her. And her . . .*

On This Day
remembering 22nd May 1981

'No more skulking indoors long winter evenings;
no more turning at every second step,
heart in your gullet even in daylight, thinking
you hear him behind you – the sudden feel of hands
on your back, your arm, your neck – his staring eyes
holding yours as you fall . . . Of course, we know,
now, how he looked – the white face, tousled hair
and sharp black beard. We didn't, then, and that
was worse, I think – these five long years of terror
when any man – even someone you knew! –
might be the one. The Yorkshire Ripper. Yes,
it was on our patch – Leeds, Bradford, Halifax –
and it seems his first attack was here, right here
in our own town . . . Well, it's over. He's caught, and tried,
and the news this evening, twenty-second of May,
is this: SUTCLIFFE SENTENCED TO THIRTY YEARS.
And surely a man who's murdered thirteen times
will never be freed? So we can breathe again.'

Yes, that was what we thought, that late-spring day
in 1981. But years of dread
don't just dissolve as the black van drives away
from the court-room, not at all. It took a while,
three summers and two winters, to relax,
to wake not fearing what the day might hold,
to stroll in the sun without a backward look,
not to send for a taxi after dark.

And still, the names – his surname; 'Garden Lane',
where he lived; or 'Alma Road', where Jacqueline
walked home each evening to her room in hall
until the night he felled her on the kerb . . .
I hear the names, and a shadow dims the sun.

Skunk, Fox

A quite indelible stench:
sunny morning, skunk on the interstate,
dead on the centre lane , not spread
but as we straddle him with caution
punishing several acres of air anyway
and still humming away at thirty yards
when we return much later.

Later, back on home ground,
fox on the M62 at midnight –
tan flash from the right, in the beam,
then the bang, not loud, then nothing.
Late, and a long day, so forward,
till the car checks, sobs to a stop.
Our footsteps meet in front, before
her sleek torso wedged fast in the grille
and stirring; heaving. Still with us.
'Awaiting rescue' we sense a curt convulsion,
shirk it. Glare of the blunt breakdown van
shows her dropped free, stretched, done for.

All through the wet tow home
she keeps pace, streaking along
taut jangling wires from where
we left her, barren at a blow,
cold-shoulder stiffening,
to me here – warm pulsing bulk
that thrusts past eye-sockets,
whams in to cram the whole gulf
of my creaking skull,
lodged here, still with me –

me her loud gleaming predator,
blinding-eyed, fast beyond nature.
The scalding spittle puckers her cheek,
the fire-breath stifles her,
an indelible stink.

Here's Love

'Here's love!' she says, waving a generous glass
of tawny, syrupy sherry. And we drink,
her daughter Ivy, Martin my cousin, and I –
her clever visiting young granddaughter,
lost daughter's daughter – at university,
which makes no odds to her. We drink. 'Here's love!'

'Whatever must you have thought of me,' she says,
'last night when I sent you to get that handkerchief
and you saw my little bottle in the drawer?
Don't you go thinking I'm a drunkard,' she says,
'it's just a teaspoonful I have, you know,
in my milk at night, that Ivy warms for me.
That gets me off. Keeps me alive till morning.'

'Ooh . . . already?' she says, when I fetch my coat –
smiling and screwing her mouth in mock-distress,
white head cocked sideways, luminous grey-green eyes
pouring concern and love. 'You wouldn't go
in one of them new carriages,' she says –
'no door to the corridor, and just one man?
And your father's going to meet you at the station?
All them dark trees,' she says. 'You get home safe.'

I did as you said, dear Gran. I got home safe.
It's what you always wanted for me – as if
by keeping away from lone men on the train,
by being escorted past those twilight trees,
I'd be preserved from every evil of life.

But came that dingy afternoon between
one Christmas and New Year's Eve: you missed your step
and fell, in the gap between your bed and Ivy's;
she wasn't home from work, and you couldn't get up.

When the doctor came you were cold, but, he said, not hurt.
They put you to bed with your faithful whisky and milk,
and it got you off a treat, as you used to say.
But then you went on a journey and didn't come back.
A generous, kindly drink: it served you well;
you died as you'd always lived – relaxed, no fuss.

I raise a glass of the best to you, Gran. Here's love.

After Summer

Midsummer, like noon, like midnight,
comes too soon for sense:
no shorts or sandals yet, not a clout cast
and it's June already, ash trees still half-naked.
Wimbledon gone, it'll start to feel *backendish*.

Scarcely into the morning, twelve o'clock strikes
and day is now descending.
The moment the red orb dips behind a hill
it's over. One day further away from birth,
one day closer to unthinkable dusk.

But revels beckon still, and the night's young yet,
or so you suppose, not yet ready for bed.
The pumpkin hour
arrives. Is past. And now the small hours loom –
three, when the spirit slips its yoke most lightly.

Afer summer, sunset, midnight – age.
'It's all down'ill from 'ere, luv.'
You're sixty and counting, well down the far slope
– as if your thirties had offered you nirvana . . .

This leaf, though – look how the light shines through its veins.

ACKNOWLEDGEMENTS

I would like to thank the editors of the following anthologies and magazines, in which some of the poems in this book have previously appeared: *Seven Ages of Woman*, edited by Toni Wilde and Heather Randall; *Hand Luggage Only*, the anthology of Open Poetry's 2007 international sonnet competition, edited by Christopher Whitby; *ARTEMISpoetry*, the magazine of the Second Light Network of Women Poets; and *About Larkin*, that of the Philip Larkin Society. I also want to thank my husband Michael Edwards for his unfailing – and unstinting – support and help in the preparation of this collection.

THE HIGH WINDOW

The following collections are also available from our website, where further information will be found:
https://thehighwindowpress.com/the-press/

A Slow Blues, New and Selected Poems by David Cooke
Angles & Visions by Anthony Costello
The Emigrant's Farewell by James W. Wood
Four American Poets edited by Anthony Costello
Dust by Bethany W. Pope
From Inside by Anthony Howell
The Edge of Seeing by John Duffy
End Phrase by Mario Susko
Bloody, proud and murderous men, adulterers and enemies of God by Steve Ely
Bare Bones by Norton Hodges
Wounded Light by James Russell
Bone Antler Stone by Tim Miller
Wardrobe Blues for a Japanese Lady by Alan Price;
Trodden Before by Patricia McCarthy
Janky Tuk Tuks by Wendy Holborow
Cradle of Bones by Frances Sackett
Of Course, the Yellow Cab by Ken Champion
Forms of Exile: Selected Poems of Marina Tsvetaeva trans. by Belinda Cooke
West South North North South East by Daniel Bennett
Surfaces by Michael Lesher
Man Walking on Water with Tie Askew by Margaret Wilmott
Songs of Realisation by Anthony Howell
Building a Kingdom, New and Selected Poems 1989-2019 by James W. Wood
The Unmaking by Tim O'Leary
Out of the Blue, Selected Poems by Wendy Klein